Big Friend, Little Friend:

A Book about Symbiosis

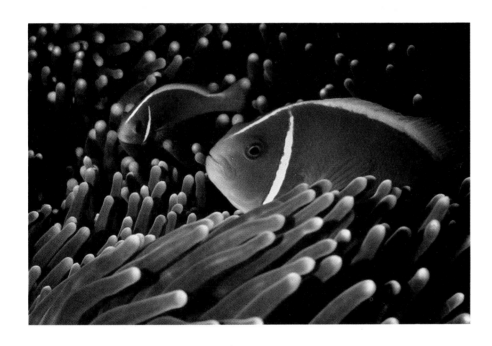

Susan Sussman and Robert James

Houghton Mifflin Company   Boston   1989

For my Chicago and California cousins,
animal lovers, all.

— S.S.

To Carolyn, with whom I have had a mutualistically
symbiotic relationship for many, many great years.

— R.J.

Library of Congress Cataloging-in-Publication Data

Sussman, Susan.
    Big friend, little friend : a book about symbiosis / Susan Sussman
and Robert James.
        p.   cm.
    Summary: Describes organisms that live together in mutual
dependence, such as the African buffalo and the red-billed oxpecker,
the protozoan and the honeyguide, the sea anemone and the boxing
crab, and the acacia bush and the ant.
    ISBN 0-395-49701-9
    1. Symbiosis—Juvenile literature. [1. Symbiosis.] I. James,
Robert, 1944– . II. Title.
QH548.S87 1989
574.5′2482—dc20   89-2127
                         CIP
                         AC

Printed in the United States of America

Y 10 9 8 7 6 5 4 3 2 1

Symbiosis

Why does the shark protect the remora fish instead of eating it? Symbiosis. Why does the red ant feed its young to the blue butterfly? Symbiosis. What makes the seeing-eye fish befriend the blind shrimp? Symbiosis.

Symbiosis is a Greek word meaning "life together." It is the word scientists use to describe the way two organisms help each other live. We see symbiosis in the lives of the tiniest ants and the biggest elephants. Sometimes two "symbionts" would die without each other. Other times they might be able to live, but would not be as healthy or as comfortable.

Studying symbiosis helps us understand some of the bizarre behavior we see in nature. There are thousands of symbiotic relationships. *Big Friend, Little Friend* looks at a few of these.

Big Friend: *African Buffalo*
Little Friend: *Red-Billed Oxpecker*

Did an insect ever bite you in a spot you couldn't reach? If so, you can understand how miserable even the largest animals are when they are bitten by tiny insects. We think of large animals as having skin too tough to be bothered by mosquitoes and flies. But although their skin is thick, it is sensitive. Fortunately, African animals have friends to help them out.

Red-billed and yellow-billed oxpeckers are often found on buffaloes, rhinoceros, elephants, antelopes, giraffes, and other large herbivores (plant-eating animals). These birds ride the backs of large animals, or hang woodpecker-style from their bodies. As they ride, the oxpeckers peck off ticks, leeches, flies, and other pests that bite and sometimes burrow into the skin of the big animals. The oxpeckers also scare off insects that might otherwise land.

Oxpeckers would die if they couldn't eat herbivore blood that has first passed through a tick. Nearly their entire life is spent on a herbivore. One of the few times oxpeckers ever leave their host is when they are startled or when they nest.

Oxpeckers have good eyesight and are extremely alert. They are usually the first to spot danger and call a warning. If a host is slow to react to the danger, the oxpecker flies to the animal's head and starts pecking and thumping on its skull.

Big Friend: *Honey Badger*
Little Friend: *Greater Honey Guide*

Imagine finding your favorite food and not being able to get to it. That is the honey guide's problem. This small African bird loves honey and is a whiz at finding honeybees' nests. Getting inside a nest, however, is not so easy.

For one thing, bees sometimes build their honeycombs in the ground, in tree trunks, or inside giant termite hills made of hard, dried dirt. The honey guide's small bill cannot peck through these tough shells. Also, the bees might sting the honey guide. When a honey guide finds a beehive, it flies off to find a honey badger.

The honey badger is a slow-moving, furry animal that loves honey but isn't good at finding it. When the badger spots the honey guide flitting, darting, and chirping, it follows, letting the honey guide lead the way to the beehive.

With its long, sharp claws, the honey badger tears into the beehive, ripping open the honeycomb. Bees cannot drive off the badger, whose thick fur coat and tough skin protect it from bee stings. When the badger has eaten its fill of honey, it waddles off. Many of the now homeless bees follow it. Soon they will build a new hive. When the bees have gone, the honey guide moves in and feasts on the honey, beeswax, and bee grubs left in the comb.

Sometimes a little friend is a big friend to an even smaller creature. The honey guide likes to eat honeycomb, but the comb is made of wax, which the bird cannot digest. The bird would die if not for its little friend, a protozoan (which means "little animal"). This animal is so

tiny you need a microscope to see it. It lives inside the honey guide's intestine. The protozoan lives on the wax the honey guide eats, changing it into matter the honey guide can pass from its body.

Big Friend: *Pygmy Falcon*
Little Friend: *Social Weaver*

The social weavers' woven nests hang like ornaments in trees throughout south and east Africa. This small bird is not at all good at defending itself. It is always in danger of being attacked and eaten by predatory birds. To protect itself, the social weaver arranges to keep a bodyguard nearby.

While weaving its nest from twigs, sticks, and grass, the weaver makes many chambers, like tiny apartments. Most of the chambers will be lived in by weavers. But one becomes the home of a pygmy falcon.

The falcon is a predatory bird. It hunts mice, birds, and other small creatures for food. Since the social weaver gives the pygmy falcon a place to live, the falcon does not harm the weaver. Instead, the falcon uses its strong curved beak and sharp talons to defend itself and its home. When other predators come near the nest, the falcon boldly drives them away.

Big Friend: *Tuatara Lizard*
Little Friend: *Giant Petrel*

The slow-moving tuatara doesn't make its own home. This reptile has two bird friends who share their homes with it.

The giant petrel and the sooty shearwater are duck-sized birds. They dig nests large enough for the tuatara. Besides giving this lizard a home, the birds eat the parasites and prickly plants that stick to the tuatara's skin.

The tuatara stays with one bird a while, eating insects and parasites that infest the nest. When that nest is clean, the tuatara moves on to another. It also defends the birds and their nests from attack.

All of the tuatara's dinosaur cousins died off around two hundred million years ago. Scientists think one reason this reptile has survived is that it lives on the tiny island of New Zealand, where it has few enemies and little competition for food.

The tuatara lives many years. It has a slow metabolic rate, which means its heart beats slowly and its cells don't wear out quickly. It does everything slowly. It is twenty years old before it first breeds. Its eggs take sixteen months to hatch. With the giant petrel and sooty shearwater to make a home for it, the tuatara has nothing to do but eat and rest. Perhaps this is one of the reasons this lizard sometimes lives for one hundred years.

Big Friend: *Gobid Fish*
Little Friend: *Blind Shrimp*

You've heard of a seeing-eye dog, but did you know there is a seeing-eye fish?

The gobid fish cares for a shrimp that is completely blind. When the shrimp wants to go somewhere, it taps the gobid and then grabs a pectoral fin (located on the side, just behind the gills) with its claw. The gobid becomes a seeing-eye fish for the shrimp.

These friends live in the sandy bottoms of the Red Sea and the Indian and Pacific oceans. There is no coral or rock where they can hunt for food. There are no places to hide from enemies. To make a home, the blind shrimp digs a large cave in the sand. It always makes the home large enough for the gobid.

The blind shrimp has never been seen living away from the gobid. It could not survive without its friend. The gobid takes the shrimp out to find food. Sometimes the blind shrimp stays home and the gobid goes out, gets food, and brings it back.

Big Friend: *White-tailed Surgeon Fish*
Little Friend: *Cleaner Shrimp*

Have you ever seen a line of cars waiting to go into a car wash? This is how different species of fish line up to wait for the cleaner shrimp, the wrasse, and other cleaner fish.

Colonies of these tiny cleaners live in all the Earth's warm oceans. When a large fish swims into the colony, the cleaners swim over and around it. They pick and eat parasites off its skin, dig out pebbles stuck in its scales, and clean between its teeth. Sometimes the cleaners must bite the fish to remove a parasite that has dug into the fish's skin.

Fish that are being cleaned show some strange behavior. Even though they are usually fierce predators, these fish never attack the cleaners. They roll over, lie on their backs or sides, and open their gills and mouths so the cleaners can do their work. Fish usually keep moving to force water through their gills so they can breathe well. But they stop moving while they are being cleaned. If a grouper is being cleaned when danger threatens, it closes its mouth to prepare to swim away. If a cleaner is inside its mouth, the grouper leaves a small opening to allow the cleaner to escape.

Fish that migrate from one place to another line up at cleaning stations along the way. Once a fish is clean, it swims off and another fish moves into its place. If there were no cleaners, the large fish would be killed by the parasites and debris lodged in their bodies. And if there were no large fish, the cleaners would not have this steady supply of food.

Big Friend: *Shark*
Little Friend: *Remora*

The remora is an underwater hitchhiker. It looks like a miniature shark but has a specially shaped suction cup on the top of its head. When a shark, ray, turtle, or other creature swims by, the remora uses the cup to stick itself onto the larger animal.

As the big fish eats, the remora releases its suction cup and swims alongside, catching and eating scraps of food. The shark offers the remora protection from other predators. It also carries the remora from one place to another. The remora repays its hosts by nibbling parasites off a fish's skin or barnacles and leeches from under a turtle's flipper.

The remora's suction is so strong that some fishermen put this suckerfish on their lines. As soon as the remora attaches itself to another fish, the fisherman reels both of them in.

Big Friend: *Giant Sea Anemone*
Little Friend: *Damselfish*

The brightly colored damselfish (also called clownfish) lives in all the warm oceans except the Atlantic. This little fish darts around, inviting larger fish to chase it. When a fish starts to follow, the damselfish quickly swims to its friend, the giant sea anemone.

The anemone is an animal but looks more like a plant. The damselfish tells the anemone a big fish is coming by rubbing against the anemone's leaflike tentacles. The poison in these tentacles stuns the big fish chasing the damselfish into the anemone. Once the fish is stunned, the damselfish eats its fill and the anemone swallows the rest.

Scientists used to think damselfish could not be harmed by the stinging cells of the anemone. We now know that each damselfish must build an immunity to its anemone. To do this, the damselfish begins by brushing lightly against one or two tentacles, then a few more. It does this until it is completely immune to the anemone's sting. But this immunity is good only for that one anemone.

A damselfish and its anemone are able to recognize each other. Some anemones have several resident damselfish and will make no move to attack any of them. But if a new damselfish wanders into the tentacles, it is stung, stunned, and eaten.

Big Friend: *Sponge Crab*
Little Friend: *Red Sponge*

Many fish in the Mediterranean Sea would eat the sponge crab if they could find it. But this crab has developed an unusual way to disguise itself. Using its sharp pincers, the crab snips off a piece from a red sponge colony. Then, with its back legs, the crab holds the sponge onto its back.

As the piece of sponge grows, it fills in the uneven spaces on the crab's shell. After about a month, the sponge stays on without being held by the crab. To fish swimming by, the crab looks like a sponge. Since fish don't eat sponges, they leave the crab alone.

This partnership is also good for the sponge. Sponges eat by sucking in water, taking what food they can find in it, and squirting the water back out. Because sponges can't move by themselves, they suck in water from the same small area over and over. After a while, there is little food left in the water near them.

When a sponge is stuck on a crab's back, it moves around with the crab. Traveling to different places means the sponge has a new supply of food all the time. Also, as the crab tears its food, bits and pieces become food for the sponge. The sponge continues to grow until it completely covers the crab's shell.

Big Friend: *Boxing Crab*
Little Friend: *Sea Anemone*

Although the boxing crab is large, its pincers aren't strong enough to hurt or drive away scaly fish. How does the crab defend itself against an attacking fish? When the boxing crab moves from place to place in the Indian Ocean, it looks for a sea anemone.

The sea anemone is a plantlike animal whose tentacles are filled with poisonous stinging cells. The crab finds a couple of small anemones and places each one on a special hook on the top of a pincer. The crab then walks along, holding the anemones out in front of it the way a prizefighter holds up boxing gloves. When an enemy approaches, the crab jabs it with one of the anemones. The anemone stings and chases off the would-be predator. Once the crab is carrying anemones on its pincers, its next set of legs grow small pincers for food gathering.

Anemones cannot move around by themselves. This can make food-finding a problem. An anemone that is carried around by a crab feasts on scraps left over by its host.

Big Friend: *Large Blue Butterfly*
Little Friend: *Red Ant*

The large blue butterfly lays its eggs on thyme plants in Europe and Asia. After an egg hatches, the new caterpillar eats the thyme leaves and grows quickly. It outgrows its skin (molts) three times. After the third molt, the caterpillar falls to the ground and wanders around as if it were confused or lost.

Red ants live in the same area. When a red ant sees a caterpillar wandering around on the ground, it returns to the nest and brings other ants. Soon many red ants dance around the caterpillar. They stroke it and push out some honeydew (sugar-water produced by the caterpillar's digestion), which they drink. Then they carry the caterpillar down into the ant city and treat it like a royal guest. They give it a soft bed and bring it food.

The most important food the ants bring is some of their own young. Although the caterpillar will eat almost any food the ants set in front of it, it will not turn into a butterfly and will die if its food doesn't include ant larvae. In return for the ants' care, the caterpillar provides the colony with a constant supply of honeydew.

As the caterpillar changes into a pupa, the ants continue to guard it and care for it. When the adult butterfly emerges from the cocoon, blood does not begin flowing into its wings. This allows the wings to stay next to the body so the butterfly can fit through the narrow passage of the ant colony. Once the butterfly is outside, blood begins flowing to the wings and they spread out. The large blue butterfly is the only butterfly in the world whose wings do not spread out the moment it leaves the cocoon.

Big Friend: *Yucca*
Little Friend: *Pronuba Moth*

The yucca plant and the pronuba moth would each die without the other. Like most plants, yuccas grow from seeds. And, in order for this Arizona desert plant to make seeds, fine powdery pollen from a stylus (the male part of the plant) must be brought to a stigma (the female part of the plant). This is called *pollination.* Pollination is most often done by wind or bees. But only the small pronuba moth can pollinate yuccas.

The pronuba moth gathers yucca flower pollen by rolling it into a ball with its specially designed mouth parts and front legs. It then flies to another flower, drops the ball of pollen into the hollow stigma, and packs it down. This pollen fertilizes the flowers, and seeds begin to grow.

In return, the yucca flower becomes a nursery for the moth's eggs. After the moth packs in the pollen, it lays about six eggs at the base of the flower. The flower makes a safe, food-filled home for the eggs. When they hatch, each pronuba caterpillar eats about twenty of the young yucca seeds. Since each flower produces around two hundred seeds, the caterpillars don't hurt the yucca plant. Some of the remaining seeds fall to the ground and grow into new plants.

Big Friend: *Acacia Bush*
Little Friend: *Ant*

The acacia bush and the ant have an unusual relationship. Many animals use plants for food, shelter, and protection. But in this case, the plant uses the animal for protection.

The acacia bush is covered with two-to three-inch thorns. These sharp, brittle thorns might keep smaller animals from eating the plant, but large plant-eaters can munch right through them. The acacia bush needs help to protect itself.

The plant produces food to attract a special ant. Sweet nectar grows at the base of each leaf. On the tip of each leaflet is a capsule called a *beltian body*, which contains protein for the ant.

As soon as an acacia seedling grows its first spines, a queen ant and a few workers move in. They hollow out thorns and live inside them. The ants spend their life cycle in the plant, eating the sweet food the acacia produces just for them. When animals such as cows try to eat the acacia, the ants attack and bite them until they go away. The ants also attack plant pests such as grasshoppers, aphids, and mealybugs, and vines that might strangle the plant.

Big Friend: *Human*
Little Friend: *Peregrine Falcon*

The peregrine falcon used to be a familiar bird of prey. But around 1910, this beautiful bird began disappearing from the American landscape. Land where falcons lived and hunted was taken over by houses, cities, factories, and other developments. Falcons began dying because they ate field mice and other animals that had eaten plants poisoned by chemicals such as DDT. Falcons that did not die laid eggs with shells so thin they broke before the chicks hatched.

Today people all over the country are trying to save this endangered species. Many programs have been begun to bring falcons into large cities and teach them to live with people. Falcons like to live in high places and seem right at home among skyscrapers, which they use like cliffs. City pigeons, mice, rats, and other small prey provide the falcons with an ample supply of food. These majestic birds can now be seen across the United States, soaring among the tall buildings and nesting on top of bridges.

In turn, people enjoy watching peregrines swooping through city streets, their great wings outstretched. In a dive, the peregrine falcon is the fastest creature on earth, flying up to 225 miles per hour. Office workers use binoculars to watch the peregrines that live on buildings around them. Peregrine hot lines are set up to receive information, such as which birds have found mates, where they are nesting, and how many eggs are in each nest. Birds adopted by cities are given names and become local celebrities. Newspapers carry stories about their health, the fights males have over mates, and the progress of newly hatched chicks.

Grateful acknowledgment is made to the following:
Raptor Research Center, University of Minnesota, p. 31;
Peter Arnold, Inc: Y. Arthus-Bertrand, p. 5, Fred Baven-
dam, p. 21, Lynn Funkhouser, p. 19; *Bruce Coleman,
Inc.:* Lee Lyon, p. 7, Peter Ward, p. 7, John Markham,
p. 11, Jeff Foott, p. 11, Jane Burton, p. 23, M. P. L.
Fogden, p. 27; *Animals Animals:* Arthur Gloor, p. 9,
Ashod Francis, p. 13, Zig Leszczynski, p. 15 and p. 17,
David Thompson, p. 25 and p. 29.